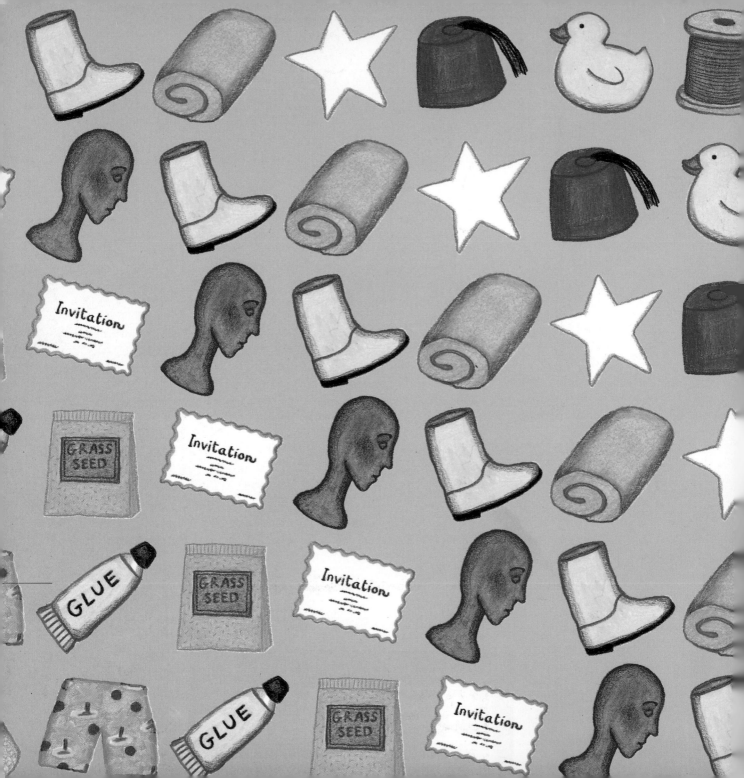

For Poppy and Rajvinder

Oxford University Press, Walton Street, Oxford OX2 6DP

Oxford New York
Athens Auckland Bangkok Bombay
Calcutta Cape Town Dar es Salaam Delhi
Florence Hong Kong Istanbul Karachi
Kuala Lumpur Madras Madrid Melbourne
Mexico City Nairobi Paris Singapore
Taipei Tokyo Toronto

and associated companies in
Berlin Ibadan

Oxford is a trade mark of Oxford University Press

Arrangement and Selection © Jill Bennett 1990
Illustrations © Nick Sharratt 1990
Reprinted 1990
First published in paperback 1992
Reprinted 1992, 1995

British Library Cataloguing in Publication Data
People poems.
  I. Bennett, Jill (Jill, Rosemary) II. Sharratt, Nick
821'.914'0809282

ISBN 0–19–276086–6 Hardback

ISBN 0–19–276110–2 Paperback

Typeset by Pentacor Ltd, High Wycombe, Bucks
Printed in Hong Kong

Acknowledgements

We are grateful for permission to include the following copyright
material in this volume.

Charles Causley, 'Charity Chadder' and 'Nicholas Naylor' from
  Early In the Morning (Viking-Kestrel). Reprinted by permission
  of David Higham Associates Limited.
Marchette Chute, 'Jemima Jane' from *Around and About*.
  Copyright 1957 by E.P. Dutton, Inc., copyright renewed 1985 by
  Marchette Chute. Reprinted by permission of Mary Chute
  Smith.
Michael Dugan, 'Ella McStumping' and 'Herbaceous Plodd' from
  My Old Dad. Reprinted by permission of Longman Cheshire Pty
  Limited.
Jean Kenward, 'Betsy Pud', © Jean Kenward 1984, first published
  in *A Very First Poetry Book*, ed. John Foster (OUP). Reprinted by
  permission of the author.
Roger McGough, 'Cousin Reggie' from *Sporting Relations* (Eyre
  Methuen & Co Ltd). Reprinted by permission of the Peters
  Fraser and Dunlop Group Ltd.
Mervyn Peake, 'My Uncle Paul of Pimlico'. Reprinted by
  permission of Maurice Michael.
Colin West, 'My Uncle is a Baronet' from *Back to Front and Back
  Again*. Reprinted by permission of Century Hutchinson Limited.

PEOPLE
POEMS

Collected by Jill Bennett
Illustrated by Nick Sharratt

OXFORD UNIVERSITY PRESS

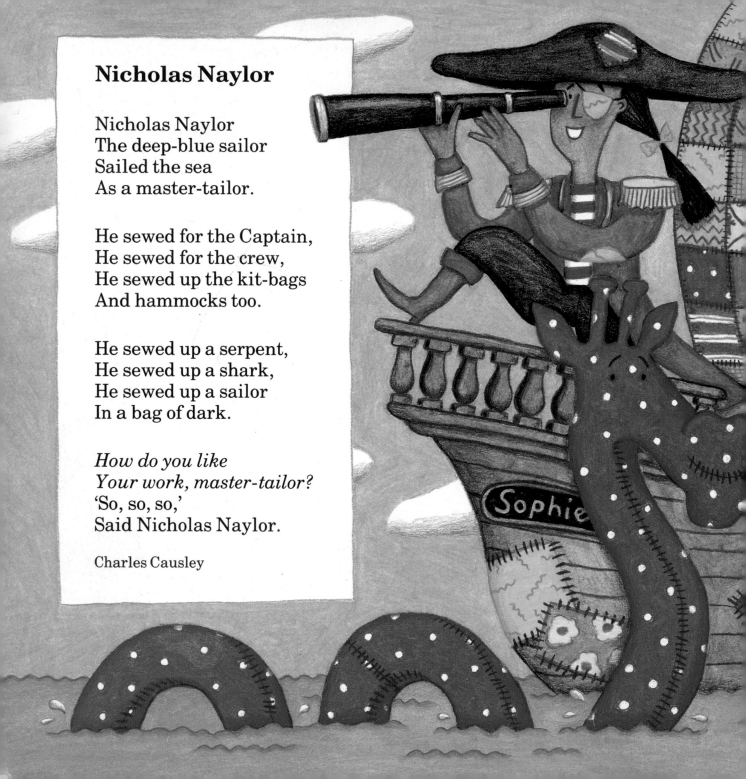

Nicholas Naylor

Nicholas Naylor
The deep-blue sailor
Sailed the sea
As a master-tailor.

He sewed for the Captain,
He sewed for the crew,
He sewed up the kit-bags
And hammocks too.

He sewed up a serpent,
He sewed up a shark,
He sewed up a sailor
In a bag of dark.

How do you like
Your work, master-tailor?
'So, so, so,'
Said Nicholas Naylor.

Charles Causley

Ella McStumping

Ella McStumping
was fond of jumping.
From tables and chairs,
bookshelves and stairs
she would jump to the floor
then climb back for more.
At the age of three
she climbed a high tree
and with one mighty cry
she leapt for the sky.
Doctor McSpetter
says she'll get better,
and the hospital say
she can come home next May,
and Ella McStumping
has given up jumping.

Michael Dugan

GO BY BUS!

My uncle is a baronet

My uncle is a baronet,
He sleeps beside the hearth,
And likes to play the clarinet
While sitting in the bath.

Colin West

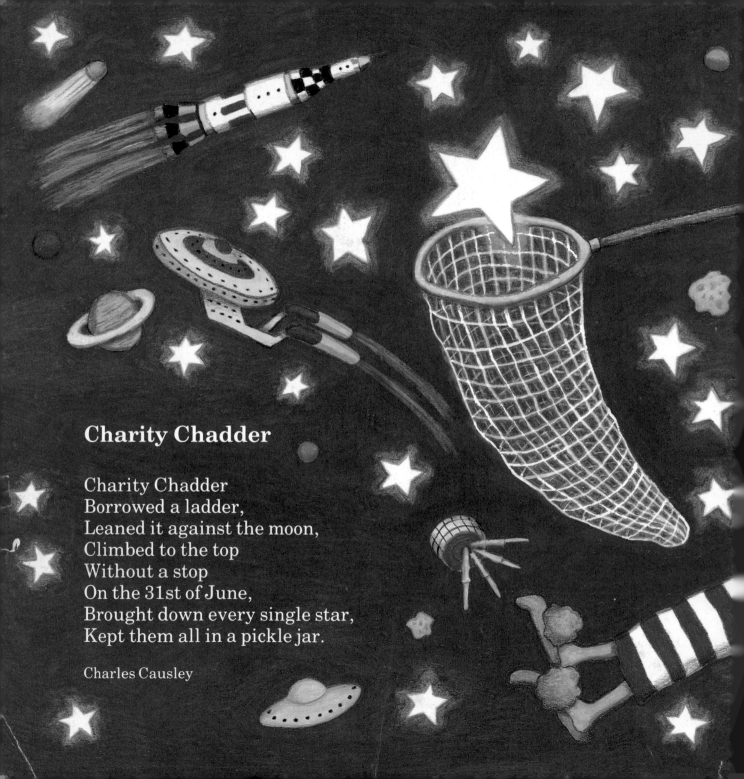

Charity Chadder

Charity Chadder
Borrowed a ladder,
Leaned it against the moon,
Climbed to the top
Without a stop
On the 31st of June,
Brought down every single star,
Kept them all in a pickle jar.

Charles Causley

Betsy Pud

Did you ever come upon
Betsy Pud?
She ate much more
than a nice girl should –
You never have seen
the like of it –
she ate until
her garters split.

Whether her work
was best or worst
she always stood
in the lunch queue, first.

Whether they liked
her ways, or not,
she licked her plate
to the last, small drop;

And then, one morning –
bless my soul! –
she wolfed the whole
of a treacle roll!

Yes, every morsel,
(wasn't it rude?)
went into the tummy
of Betsy Pud;

There wasn't a fraction,
wasn't a crumb
for anyone else
who cared to come,

And Betsy swelled
at such a rate, OH!
She up and burst
like a baked potato!

What a disaster!
What a sin!
They had to bring
the hoover in,

And off she went in it.
Nobody should
be quite so greedy
as Betsy Pud.

Jean Kenward

Gregory Griggs

Gregory Griggs, Gregory Griggs,
Had twenty–seven different wigs.
He wore them up, he wore them
    down,
To please the people of the town;
He wore them east, he wore them
    west
But he never could tell which he
    loved the best.

anon.

There was a young farmer of Leeds

There was a young farmer of Leeds
Who swallowed six packets of seeds,
    It soon came to pass
    He was covered with grass,
And he couldn't sit down for the weeds.

anon.

Cousin Reggie

Cousin Reggie
who adores the sea
lives in the Midlands
unfortunately.

He surfs down escalators
in department stores
and swims the High Street
on all of his fours.

Sunbathes on the pavement
paddles in the gutter
(I think our Reggie's
a bit of a nutter).

Roger McGough

Jemima Jane

Jemima Jane,
    Oh, Jemima Jane,
She loved to go out
    And slosh in the rain.
She loved to go out
    And get herself wet,
And she had a duck
    For her favourite pet.

Every day
    At half-past four
They'd both run out
    The kitchen door;
They'd find a puddle,
    And there they'd stay
Until it was time
    To go away.

They got quite wet,
    But they didn't mind;
And every rainy
    Day they'd find
A new way to splash
    Or a new way to swim.
And the duck loved Jane,
    And Jane loved him.

Marchette Chute

My Uncle Paul
of Pimlico

My Uncle Paul of Pimlico
Has seven cats as white as snow,
Who sit at his enormous feet
And watch him, as a special treat,
Play the piano upside-down,
In his delightful dressing-gown;
The firelight leaps, the parlour glows,
And, while the music ebbs and flows,
They smile (while purring the refrains),
At little thoughts that cross their brains.

Mervyn Peake

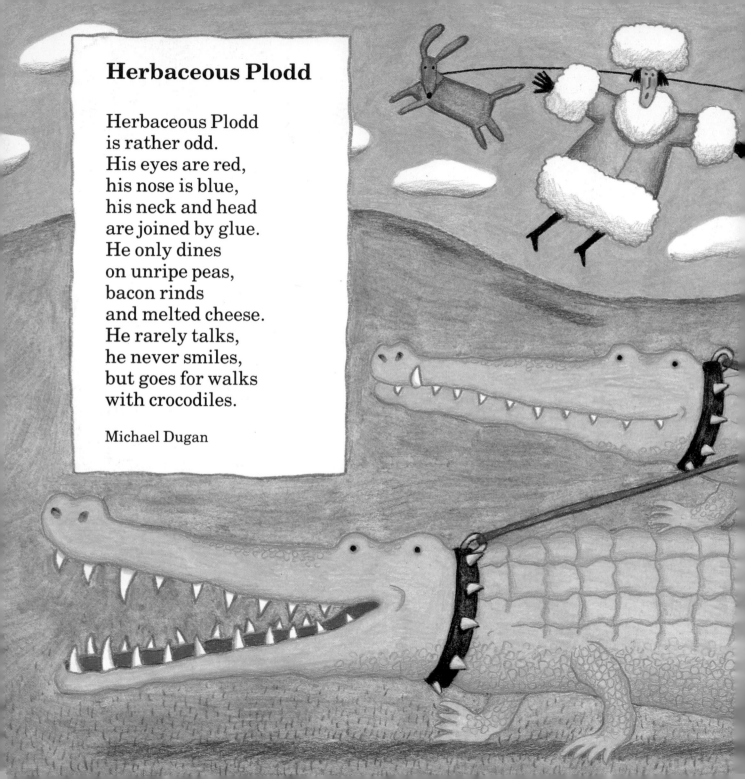

Herbaceous Plodd

Herbaceous Plodd
is rather odd.
His eyes are red,
his nose is blue,
his neck and head
are joined by glue.
He only dines
on unripe peas,
bacon rinds
and melted cheese.
He rarely talks,
he never smiles,
but goes for walks
with crocodiles.

Michael Dugan

An old woman sat spinning

An old woman sat spinning
And that's the beginning.
She had a calf
And that's half.
And she went to a ball,
And that's all.

trad.

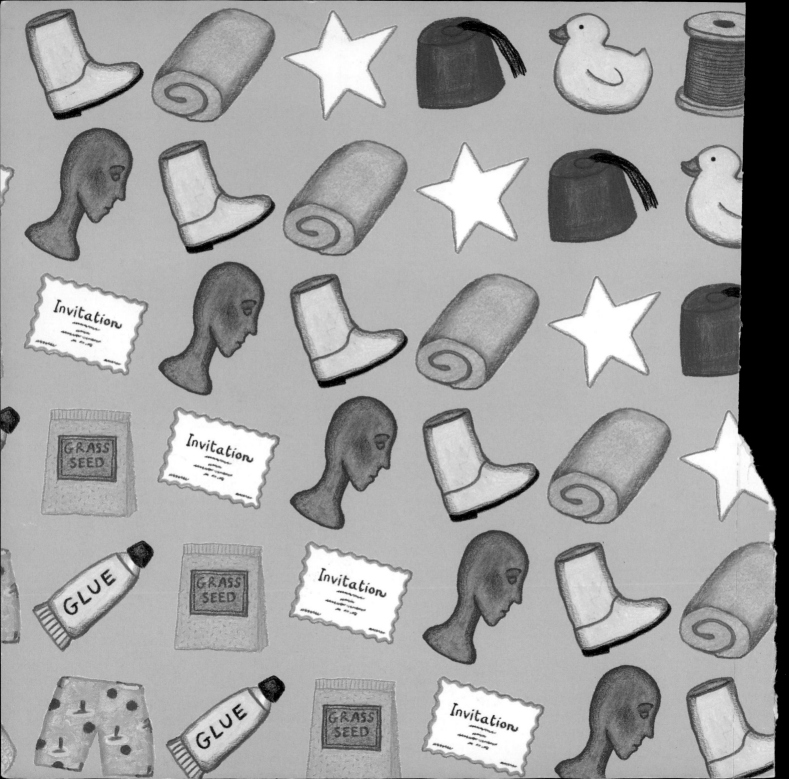